Outdoor Education: Beyond the Classroom Walls

Thomas J. Rillo

**PHI DELTA KAPPA
EDUCATIONAL FOUNDATION**

THOMAS J. RILLO

Thomas J. Rillo is a professor in the School of Health, Physical Education, and Recreation at Indiana University. He also has taught at Montclair State College and Glassboro State College, both in New Jersey, and at Southern Illinois University.

Rillo has been active in the field of outdoor education for more than 35 years. He has served as a consultant to many school systems in setting up outdoor education programs and has published widely in the field. He serves as consulting editor for the *Journal of Environmental Education, Science Activities Magazine*, and *The Communicator — New York State Journal of Outdoor Education*.

In 1970 Rillo received the New Jersey Conservation Educator of the Year Award, sponsored by the National Wildlife Federation. In 1980 he received a Distinguished Teaching Award from Indiana University.

Series Editor, Derek L. Burleson

Outdoor Education: Beyond the Classroom Walls

by
Thomas J. Rillo

Library of Congress Catalog Card Number 85-61789
ISBN 0-87367-232-1
Copyright © 1985 by the Phi Delta Kappa Educational Foundation
Bloomington, Indiana

This fastback is sponsored by the Indiana University Chapter of Phi Delta Kappa, which made a generous contribution toward publication costs. The chapter sponsors this fastback to honor the memory of the late Robert W. Tully, who died on 12 June 1981.

Bob Tully was an understanding teacher, gentle counselor, and a dedicated administrator at Indiana University for 26 years. He was also an ordained minister in the Church of the Brethren. His faith was reflected in his service to anyone who needed help.

Bob Tully was an early leader in the camping and outdoor education movement. He helped to develop Bradford Woods, Indiana University's 2,300-acre outdoor education laboratory, and conducted several regional conferences and institutes on camping and outdoor education. His professional contributions brought him honors at both state and national levels.

His love of nature and the outdoors and his contributions to camping and outdoor education make this fastback a most appropriate memorial.

Table of Contents

What Is Outdoor Education? 7

Methods in Outdoor Education 9
  Small-Group Instruction 9
  References and Resources for Outdoor Education 10
  Preparing to Teach Outdoors 10

Starting an Outdoor Education Program 12
  Role of the Outdoor Education Committee 12
  Selecting an Outdoor Education Program 12

Correlating Outdoor Education with the School Curriculum 15
  Curriculum Approaches to Outdoor Education 15
  Correlating Outdoor Education with Specific Subjects 16

Evaluating Outdoor Education 25

Summing Up 26

Resources 28

What Is Outdoor Education?

A simple but precise definition of outdoor education has been provided by the late Lloyd Burgess Sharp, an early leader in the field, who said:

> In simple terms, outdoor education means all of that learning included in the curriculum in any subject matter area and at any grade level which can best be learned outside the classroom.

Sharp also described outdoor education as "a commonsense method of learning. It is natural, plain, and direct."

The subject matter of outdoor education is selected through an analysis of the curriculum to determine where learning can best take place — inside or outside the classroom. As Sharp explains:

> That which ought and can best be taught inside the schoolroom should there be taught, and that which can best be learned through experience, dealing directly with native materials and life situations outside the school, should there be learned.

Sharp's definition of outdoor education implies that it is not a separate subject in itself, but rather includes content from several areas of the curriculum — content that is best learned outside the classroom.

Outdoor education can begin as soon as students and teachers step beyond the classroom door. It can take place on the school steps, the sidewalk, the school yard, the playground, a nearby park, or other areas in the community. The outdoor activity may be short term, as short as five minutes, a half hour, or an hour. Or it may include an overnight experience at a camping facility or last as long as a week. This is commonly referred to as resident outdoor education.

The basic methods of effective outdoor learning are observation, research, and reflection. Direct observation arouses interest, curiosity, and the desire for investigation. Research involves the use of references to learn more about the phenomena experienced in the outdoors. Reflection provides a time for the assimilation of what has been learned in terms of understandings and appreciation.

Many teachers think that they are not adequately prepared to teach in the outdoors. They think that one has to be a naturalist, geologist, botanist, zoologist, herpetologist, ornithologist, entomologist, ichthyologist, lichenologist, ecologist, or conservationist in order to teach students in the outdoors. Although it would be wonderful to be proficient in all of these fields, realistically this is not possible. Teachers' lack of technical background in these sciences should not deter them from providing students direct experiences in the outdoors. However, this is not to say that teachers do not need to acquire some technical background. But they do not need to be specialists in the fields.

Methods in Outdoor Education

In outdoor education many questions arise over how much the teacher should tell students and what students should discover for themselves. Some have estimated that as many as 80% of the questions raised by students can be answered by the students themselves. It is the writer's opinion that learning by discovery is the most appropriate method in outdoor education. We should give all students the opportunity to arrive at answers by themselves. Certainly, in the outdoors much of the data needed for answering questions can be attained through direct observation using all the senses.

The essence of the discovery method in outdoor education is knowing how to arouse curiosity. This is much more important than knowing the answers. A teacher will never know the answers to all the questions asked during an outdoor education experience. The discovery approach to learning requires that teachers first arouse curiosity and then direct students to the resources to satisfy that curiosity. Finding out what is *not* known is the important thing. Leading students to discovery by questioning rather than by telling is an effective technique, whether in the classroom or in the outdoor laboratory.

Learning by discovery leads students to develop concepts from concrete experiences. Learning by discovery through direct experience is not new. Over 300 years ago, Comenius wrote that his objective was "to seek and find a method by which teachers teach less and learners learn more." Outdoor education provides the setting in which the students learn to find out things for themselves.

Small-Group Instruction

In outdoor education it is important that instruction is conducted in small groups so that each individual will have the opportunity to use all five senses.

Every member of the group should have the opportunity to look, touch, smell, hear, and taste while exploring phenomena in the outdoors. The way to ensure that each individual becomes involved is through small-group instruction.

References and Resources for Outdoor Education

Part of learning by discovery is knowing where and how to look for answers. Often one question leads to another, and one answer leads to another question. When students are curious and seek answers, a teacher will need to have resources readily available for students to find answers to their questions.

The reference books and resource materials used in the outdoor education program should be area specific and at the proper reading level for the age group in the program. A collection of reference materials should be available at both the school and the field sites where outdoor education is conducted. Some schools have an outdoor education center where the reference collection is housed. The school and classroom library should also contain books, pamphlets, and periodicals pertaining to the topics covered in the outdoor education program. A relatively recent development has been the use of trailers or vans filled with reference and resource materials. These serve as mobile reference units for use at school sites, in a nearby park, in the community, or at a resident outdoor education center.

Reference and resource materials are needed for the investigating component of outdoor education. These materials give students access to what is already known. They help the student to systematize what has been learned from direct experience.

Regardless of the method used, the basic principle of outdoor education is direct experience, which helps students to gain a deeper understanding of life around them, which shows the interrelatedness of things in the natural environment, and which develops an appreciation of people's interdependence with the physical world.

Preparing to Teach Outdoors

Outdoor education will not be integrated into the curriculum until teachers themselves are introduced to the possibilities for its use. Not only should teachers be taught how to use the outdoors to enhance their teaching but also should have personal experiences in the outdoors as part of their teacher education program. Preservice and inservice teachers should have the opportunity to enroll in courses that include field experiences in the outdoors. For preservice teachers a practicum in outdoor teaching should be scheduled prior to student teaching so that they can experiment with the direct experience methods as well as with other methods they have studied in the college classroom.

A good example of an outdoor education teacher-training program is the one conducted by Northern Illinois University. Students take three or four courses in a block sequence, thereby freeing themselves for a variety of outdoor experiential learning-teaching situations at the Lorado Taft Field Campus. This program gives the students an opportunity to learn and teach in an outdoor setting for at least two weeks, where they work with elementary school students.

Another program preparing preservice teachers for outdoor education is conducted at the New Jersey State School of Conservation, administered by Montclair State College. This program originated as a result of a mandate requiring all sophomores at the New Jersey state colleges (which were state teachers colleges at that time) to experience one week at the School of Conservation, regardless of their education major. Currently it is an optional program open to all students attending the eight state colleges in New Jersey.

Starting an Outdoor Education Program

Historically, outdoor education programs have been initiated through the interest and dedication of a single individual or a small group committed to the idea that the outdoors provides a rich climate for extending and enriching the curriculum. More recently, as outdoor education programs have become better established, a standing committee is used to plan and maintain the program.

Role of the Outdoor Education Committee

The outdoor education committee should include persons representing parents, students, teachers, administrators, and the board of education. Additional members might include those with special expertise, such as the school system's legal counsel, the school architect, and non-school resource persons. The responsibilities of this committee are: 1) establishing the need, 2) articulating a philosophy and goals, 3) planning the curriculum, 4) collecting resources and preparing materials, 5) arranging for inservice programs for teachers, and 6) evaluating the outdoor education program.

Selecting an Outdoor Education Program

In planning an outdoor education program, the committee needs to consider the various types of programs it may want to implement. Ultimately, the decision will depend on the curriculum goals sought and the human and material resources available.

The first type of program is referred to as *resident* or *long-term* and includes living in an outdoor setting. Usually this involves taking an entire class and the teacher from a self-contained classroom to an outdoor education site for an intensive week of study. Many school systems have found this type to be the most worthwhile in terms of the time, effort, and cost that go into the program. Resident outdoor education programs are usually a permanent part of the curriculum.

A second type of program is *day-long* or *short-term*. This includes all-day trips, field trips, individual research investigations, work projects, and club activities that are an extension of the regular academic program. The advantages of this type of program are minimum cost to the student and no need for overnight provisions. Transportation, teaching materials, and instructional staff are the main costs to the school system. Teachers can use this type of program at various times throughout the year.

A third type of program is referred to as *recreational* and is not generally associated with academic studies. Included in this category are weekend outings, overnight campouts, meetings of various interest groups, or a summer program with a recreation emphasis.

A fourth type of program is in the area of *cultural* and *aesthetic enrichment*. Here the outdoors provides a suitable setting for performance in music, drama, dance, and other performing arts activities.

If a school system decides to establish a resident outdoor education program, the organizational issues are much more complex. Consideration must be given to capital outlay for the site, logistics for transporting and housing students, and providing both instructional and support staff, as well as the type of program offered.

The program may be academic-centered, camp-centered, or a combination of the two. Academic-centered programs are closely related to the ongoing curriculum with the classroom teacher serving as the primary resource person. There is less emphasis on recreational activities and living in the outdoors. Camp-centered programs provide for more incidental kinds of learning not necessarily related to classroom work. Much time is devoted to outdoor living skills such as outdoor cooking, building shelters, and nature study. Usually specially trained staff operate the program for the students and their teachers.

Both types of programs provide valuable learning experiences. Of course, elements of both types of programming can be combined. Probably most school systems will lean in the direction of the academic-centered program because it is more in keeping with the school's instructional role and because many students have other opportunities for camping experiences.

Whatever type of outdoor education program a school system adopts, the experiences provided should:

1. Enrich and supplement the regular curriculum with activities not ordinarily available in the classroom.
2. Stress student participation in planning, executing, and evaluating.
3. Permit students to work in an informal atmosphere and with considerable flexibility in the structuring of activities.
4. Emphasize the use of natural surroundings and materials indigenous to the area.
5. Emphasize concepts, generalizations, and cause-effect relationships that integrate content across the curriculum.
6. Emphasize observation using all the senses, investigation, and speculation as a means of verification (scientific method).
7. Motivate students through questions and discussions to discover answers for themselves.
8. Have an affective dimension that develops aesthetic appreciations for the wonders in nature.

Correlating Outdoor Education with the School Curriculum

The vast outdoor setting, always available for discovery and exploration, provides the curriculum for the outdoor education program. From plans developed in the classroom, students and teachers embark on an adventure into the outdoor classroom. Through experiences gained in the outdoors, students pursue further study back in the classroom. Thus, the outdoor experience grows out of the classroom and leads back to the classroom.

Curriculum Approaches to Outdoor Education

There are various curriculum approaches to outdoor education. The *vertical articulation* approach uses a broad theme or basic understanding that is introduced at the kindergarten level and then spirals upward through each grade level and subject matter area with increasing refinement and sophistication. For example, the broad theme might be, "All living things are interdependent and interrelated." At each grade level, concepts related to this theme are explored and extended through outdoor education activities. The *horizontal articulation* approach is used to correlate outdoor activities with subject matter in grades K through 12. Subject matter is analyzed in terms of basic concepts and outdoor activities are then correlated with basic concepts of each discipline taught.

Another approach is called *modular*, which uses packaged instructional modules or planned units of study available from a variety of sources. One example of these modules is the *Outdoor Biology Instructional Strategies* (OBIS), which is designed for 10- to 15-year-old students to conduct biological investigations on the playground, in local parks, on vacant lots, and in and around neighborhood streams, ponds, or lakes. Another module example called *Acclimatization* has been developed by Steve Van Matre. Organized around a sensory, perceptual approach to ecological understanding, this program provides activities for six days of one-hour sessions per day to "acclimatize" students to their environment.

Still another modular approach is one developed by the Western Regional Environmental Education Council and the American Forest Institute called *Project Learning Tree*. These materials include K through 12 outdoor learning activities. The activities are presented in lesson plan format and can be implemented easily by the teacher. *Project Wild*, an interdisciplinary environmental and conservation education program for K through 12, also uses a lesson plan format and can be taught easily by the inexperienced outdoor educator.

An innovative modular program that appeals to both students and teachers is one called *Green Box*. Using a game-like format with DO, THINK, and SHOW cards, this program is easily implemented by the classroom teacher.

The National Environmental Education Development (NEED) program, developed in the early Seventies by the National Park Service, the National Education Association, and the Association of Classroom Teachers, has endured the test of time. This environmental awareness program is organized around five thematic strands or major concepts from the natural world. The strands are: 1) Variety and Similarities, 2) Patterns, 3) Interaction and Interdependence, 4) Continuity and Change, and 5) Adaptation and Evolution.

The packaged or modular approach is very popular with recreation departments and park systems, which do not have the time to tailor a program for each visiting group of students. It is less time consuming to implement than the horizontal or vertical articulation approach, but it does not allow for the careful curriculum correlation afforded by the other two approaches.

Correlating Outdoor Education with Specific Subjects

Outdoor education can be correlated with all subjects in the curriculum. The opportunities for studying science are unlimited, but it should not dominate the outdoor education program. In this section are suggestions for enriching all areas of the curriculum through outdoor activity.

Social Studies. Social studies teaches about the interactions of human beings with their environment. Outdoor education can provide many stimulating learning situations in which students can explore the influence of human occupancy on the local landscape, learn about local history, and come to understand the importance of conservation of natural resources. Students can observe environmental problems directly and participate in activities to eliminate such problems. The skills of problem solving and critical thinking so vital in the social studies can be put into practice in the outdoor laboratory.

Some suggested outdoor social studies activities are:

1. Exploring an old cemetery.
2. Exploring a deserted farm.
3. Exploring fencerows and other boundary markers.
4. Investigating a region for earlier human occupancy.
5. Examining tree rings and plotting them with historical events.
6. Interviewing elders of the community and tape recording the interview.
7. Interviewing an artisan in the community.
8. Writing a cultural journal similar to *Foxfire*.
9. Exploring an old Indian occupation site.
10. Exploring sites of early industries of the community.
11. Exploring former transportation sytems such as an old railroad track bed.
12. Developing a land-use map for the community.
13. Writing letters to legislators concerning environmental problems.
14. Role playing the problems of early settlers.
15. Making an inventory of pioneer "green medicine" sources.
16. Making maps of a community's historical landmarks.
17. Taking a field trip to a farm where crop rotation, contour farming, and other methods of conserving land are practiced.
18. Dramatizing in pictures, stories, and skits what humans can do to preserve wildlife.
19. Charting the historical changes in the community showing how inventions and technology have affected the economy and lifestyle.
20. Making graphs and maps to show the changing population patterns in the community.

Music. The outdoors offers many opportunities for activities that support the school music program. Students come to understand the origins of music when they learn that the first instrument was probably a hollow bone or a hollow log. Crude drums made from hollow logs, reed tubes, and taut strings stretched on a board probably formed the first band. As these primitive instruments became more refined they evolved into the components of the modern orchestra: percussion, winds, and strings. Students can explore sound-producing materials found in the outdoors much as primitive people did.

Music also can be a vital part of the group experience in outdoor education. The dining hall or around the campfire are favorite settings for group singing. Students should be introduced to folk songs, round songs, and other kinds of part singing. Eurythmics is another group participation musical activity that can be conducted in a large grassy area.

A song leader should be designated to coordinate and lead the singing. This person should be responsible for selecting the songs and teaching them. A set of song books should be available.

Some suggested music activities are:

1. Square dancing, simple folk dancing, and Indian dancing.
2. Recording sounds of streams, waterfalls, rustling leaves, birds, insects, and frogs.
3. Constructing and playing instruments made of natural materials, such as a hollow log drum, willow or basswood whistles, and wooden flutes.
4. Experimenting with the sounds produced by such materials as pebbles, acorn caps, seed pods, rocks, tree branches, and hollow reeds.
5. Listening to a variety of bird songs and interpreting the moods expressed in their music.
6. Choreographing the gaits of mammals or flight patterns of birds.
7. Making shadowgraphs to accompany songs.
8. Listening to sounds of footsteps on various surfaces such as gravel, asphalt pavement, wooden bridges, sand, grass, or snow.
9. Striking various objects to produce different tones.
10. Composing songs about things in nature such as flowers, birds, clouds, and the wind.
11. Group singing in large groups, small groups, or song festivals.
12. Dramatizing folk songs or ballads.

13. Listening to recorded music and relating it to those sounds found in the outdoors.
14. Making collections of folk songs, spirituals, ballads, vesper songs, lullaby songs, work songs, novelty songs, and national songs from other countries for use by future groups in the outdoor education program.

Language Arts. Many productive language arts activities can grow out of an outdoor education program, particularly in the areas of creative writing and oral expression. Outdoor activities provide a host of experiences on which students can draw to express their thoughts and feelings in prose and poetry. Students are motivated to write when they have had enjoyable experiences they want to share with others. Planting a tree, a trip to a quarry, exploring a cave, finding constellations in the sky are all experiences that stimulate expression of genuine thought and feelings.

Vocabulary development is a natural outgrowth of experiences in the outdoors. New words quickly become a part of students' working vocabularies because the words are used repeatedly when investigating natural phenomena. Keeping a vocabulary list and taking notes are common language arts activities in the outdoor education program. The skills of listening, speaking, reading, and writing can all be reinforced through experiences in the outdoors.

Some suggested language arts activities are:

1. Role playing animals in nature.
2. Writing nature poetry in such forms as haiku, cinquain, diamante, and tanka.
3. Writing creative stories.
4. Using similes and metaphors to describe natural phenomena.
5. Taking notes in the field and keeping lists.
6. Writing diaries or logs.
7. Writing letters to legislators and newspaper editors.
8. Telling ghost stories around a campfire.
9. Using the outdoor education reference library to look up facts.
10. Making charts, posters, and bulletin board displays.
11. Reading about the local history of the area and writing a "then and now" expository essay.

12. Giving a persuasive talk to convince the public of the need to protect the natural environment.

Mathematics. Many mathematical or geometric patterns are found in nature: in the symmetry of leaves and flower petals, in mineral and snowflake crystals, in the bees' honeycomb, and in the coloration patterns of mammals, reptiles, and insects. Pointing out these mathematical patterns in nature makes students realize that there is more to mathematics than just numbers.

Mathematics also can be used in the outdoors for a variety of measurement problems. Learning how to measure area, volume, and distance can be done much more effectively when presented with a real problem in the outdoors. Comparisons can be made among objects as to height, size, and distance. The students can count, measure, estimate, and draw scale maps.

Some suggested mathematics outdoor activities are:

1. Estimating distance by the pace method.
2. Estimating distance using triangulation.
3. Estimating heights of trees, buildings, and telephone poles using a clinometer or isosceles triangle.
4. Estimating volume of water flowing in a stream.
5. Estimating the degree of a slope.
6. Measuring an acre of land.
7. Cruising timber to estimate merchantable lumber.
8. Comparing temperature readings in various locations.
9. Identifying geometric shapes in nature.
10. Contour mapping of a lake or pond bottom.
11. Using arrangement of leaves to teach fractions.
12. Orienting using a map and compass.
13. Using body parts (foot, arm, finger) as a basis for measurement.
14. Using sight level to determine land rise or fall.
15. Finding number bases in nature such as the number of needles in a bunch on a pine tree, the number of legs on an insect, the number of points on an oak leaf.
16. Timing the travel rates of mammals, reptiles, and insects.

Science. Science educators have been using the outdoor laboratory to extend their classroom teaching for many years. The scientific method taught in the classroom is directly applicable to investigation and problem solving in the outdoors. Natural science with an emphasis on ecology provides the academic content for most outdoor education programs. Many outdoor programs use the living environment as a central theme.

Two guiding principles for studying science in the outdoors are that method is more important than fact and that generalizations are more important than facts. Using the scientific method, students can arrive at generalizations that help them to understand relationships in nature. The scientific method involves the following steps:

1. Identifying the problem.
2. Gathering preliminary data.
3. Making hypotheses based on preliminary data.
4. Stating assumptions.
5. Gathering pertinent data to test the hypothesis.
6. Accepting, modifying, or rejecting the hypothesis.
7. Drawing conclusions and making recommendations.

Some suggested outdoor science activities are:

1. Studying plant succession from meadow to forest.
2. Conducting soil tests for mineral content, compactness.
3. Predicting weather using meteorological data.
4. Conducting a quadrat or transect study to discover the ecological composition of a small area.
5. Studying pond ecology.
6. Studying the incidence of various plant life.
7. Conducting microclimate studies.
8. Monitoring water turbidity.
9. Conducting a study of animal population density.
10. Trapping small animals and insects live for study purposes.
11. Studying animal homes.
12. Scouting stumps to analyze tree rings.
13. Studying ecology of rotted logs.
14. Exploring fencerows.
15. Studying vacant lots.
16. Developing an interpretive nature trail.
17. Identifying trees by physical characteristics.
18. Constructing a terrarium or aquarium.

Health and Physical Education. Living and playing in an outdoor setting call for special attention to health and safety practices. Health and safety knowledge is important for many activities, such as proper dress for cross-country skiing, appropriate equipment for an overnight hike, adequate footwear for a marsh exploration, warm clothing to prevent hypothermia, use of first aid for severe cuts or bone breaks, and cardiovascular fitness for strenuous outdoor activity. Menu planning and food preparation in the outdoors are good experiences for teaching nutrition and proper sanitary practices.

The outdoor laboratory provides many opportunities for activities that correlate with physical education, as well as with other areas of the curriculum. For example, in learning how to play Indian games and to do Indian dances, students might do research on Indian society in the social studies class; the home economics class might make the costumes; and the industrial arts class might make the equipment to play the games.

Since so much of the outdoor education program involves physical activity, there is less need for a structured physical education program. Rather, the emphasis should be on such activities as hiking, backpacking, cross-country skiing, and physical games. These are activities that can become lifetime leisure pursuits.

Still another aspect of physical education in an outdoor education program is high adventure activities. Stress-challenge activities are becoming an important component of outdoor education programs and include such things as ropes courses, circuit training courses, initiative games, "new" games, backpacking, rock climbing, cross-country skiing, white-water canoeing, kayaking, rafting, and tubing. These challenging activities test the physical potential of students and build confidence in their abilities.

Some suggested health and physical education activities are:

1. Performing round or square dances and Indian dances.
2. Playing group initiative games.
3. Practicing outdoor safety, such as how to dress for a hike.
4. Learning first-aid techniques.
5. Rappelling or descending by rope.
6. Participating in a confidence or ropes course.
7. Playing games with native materials.
8. Planning an outdoor food menu.

9. White-water rafting, canoeing, or kayaking.
10. Constructing a rope suspension bridge.
11. Running an orienteering course.
12. Building a fitness training trail with native materials.
13. Constructing shelters with native materials.
14. Planning and participating in a backpack trip.
15. Participating in community service projects, such as cleaning a park and constructing check dams or water bars for erosion control.
16. Participating in housekeeping chores, such as cleaning sleeping areas, making beds, setting tables, and washing dishes.
17. Practicing and reinforcing personal health habits, such as brushing teeth, washing with soap and water, monitoring pulse rate, checking bood pressure, washing hands after using the latrine, etc.
18. Stalking wild animals.
19. Playing indigenous North American games, such as the Indian game of lacrosse.
20. Learning skills associated with hobbies, such as fly casting and angling, skin and scuba diving, cave exploration, lapidary, outdoor photography, archery, boating, winter sports, and outdoor survival.

Art. The outdoor education program offers unlimited opportunities for creative expression through various media and techniques. Firsthand experiences in the outdoors appeal to the senses and to the emotions. Inspiration for artistic expression flows readily from experiences in such forms as photography, sketching, modeling, and painting. Also the natural environment offers many native materials to use in art activities.

Some suggested art activities are:
1. Sketching with pencil, crayon, charcoal, or chalk.
2. Sketching clouds on plexiglass with grease pencil.
3. Modeling with native clay.
4. Making a color chart using native materials.
5. Dyeing wool using native materials.
6. Tombstone rubbings.
7. Spatter printing with toothbrushes.
8. Pencil rubbings of various textures found outdoors.
9. Weaving with native materials such as bark fibers.

10. Constructing collages, mobiles, and stabiles with native materials.
11. Making plaster-of-Paris casts.
12. Making spore prints.
13. Twig sketching in sand or snow.
14. Using blueprint paper to reproduce designs of natural objects.
15. Making shadow pattern designs.
16. Looking for designs in nature such as a circle, two half circles, zigzags, waves, or spirals.
17. Working with an outdoor kiln.
18. Creating textile designs from outdoor motifs and applying to cloth by stencils, appliqué, or batik.

Evaluating Outdoor Education

The outdoor education program should be evaluated just as other parts of the curriculum are evaluated. Although there are similarities to classroom learning in overall objectives, there are essential differences in purpose, the nature of experiences, and the amount of time involved. Therefore, the evaluation should focus on the specific objectives of the outdoor program.

A short-term program such as a field trip or even a five-day resident outdoor education experience cannot be assessed by the same criteria that are used to measure academic achievement over an entire school year. Evaluating the impact of outdoor education must focus on a broader range of behaviors than just cognitive development. The focus should be on the personal meaning the outdoor experience had for the individual student, including appreciation of and heightened sensitivity to the natural world, discovery of new interests, acquisition of new skills, learning to live in a group situation, accepting personal responsibility for the environment, as well as cognitive growth in understanding new concepts.

Instruments or procedures to evaluate these outcomes include: 1) interest inventories, 2) student narrative logs, 3) attitude scales, 4) subjective reports, 5) anecdotal records, 6) conferences, 7) interviews, 8) student opinion surveys, 9) community opinion surveys, and 10) professional opinions. Whatever method or combination of methods is used to evaluate the outdoor education program, all involved in the program should participate in the evaluation: students, teachers, administrators, parents, and other community members. If an outdoor education program is worth implementing, it deserves to be evaluated. In fact, it must be evaluated if it is to become a permanent part of the total school curriculum.

Summing Up

The premise of this fastback is that outdoor education should be an integral part of the total school curriculum. In order for young people to know about their environment, to identify problems concerning the use of natural resources, to seek alternative solutions to environmental problems, and to be committed to taking action to alleviate these problems, they must first have an experiential foundation on which to base their decisions. This foundation can be built through outdoor education. The subject matter in the regular academic program is the vehicle by which basic concepts and broad understandings of the natural environment are learned.

Outdoor education is vital to our time. As our society becomes more leisure oriented, more time will be available. Students, indeed all citizens, can make worthy use of this leisure time through purposeful, recreative outdoor experiences. As our cities and towns become more crowded, the need to escape to open space and to a cleaner environment becomes extremely important. Young people today are the decision makers of tomorrow. As they plan the living environments of the future, their outdoor education background will help them to make plans that are in harmony with the natural environment. What greater contribution can any education program provide than to make the living space about us a quality environment, not for just human beings but for all forms of life?

It does not take a great expenditure of funds to start an outdoor education program. What is needed first is the interest and dedication of a few educators who are able to articulate the philosophy of outdoor education and show how it is in harmony with the overall philosophy of the school system. Out of this effort will come guiding principles and operational policies that give direction to the outdoor education program.

Correlating outdoor education activities with the basic curriculum is both easy and necessary. By using an interdisciplinary approach the curriculum is both extended and enriched. A student-centered approach should be used when teaching in the outdoors.

The outdoor education program can be conducted at a variety of learning sites. No two outdoor education programs need to be the same. Geographical differences, socio-cultural differences, and community resource differences may dictate programs that are quite different from one another.

The importance of evaluation is self-evident. Stated objectives need to be evaluated if the program is to grow and develop. Continued evaluation will ensure that the program will meet special needs.

If education can be defined as a search for meaning, then outdoor education is the place to begin. It is time to get started. This fastback should help you begin.

Resources

Books

Bachert, Russell E., and Snooks, Emerson L. *Outdoor Education Equipment*. Danville, Ill.: Interstate Printers and Publishers, 1974.

Brainerd, John. *Working with Nature*. New York: Oxford University Press, 1973.

Comstock, Anna B. *Handbook of Nature Study*. Ithaca, N.Y.: Comstock Publishing Associates, 1963.

Cornell, Joseph B. *Sharing Nature with Children*. Nevada City, Calif.: Amanda, 1979.

Couchman, Kenneth J., et al. *Examining Your Environment Series*. 12 volumes. Distributed by Winston Press, Minneapolis, Minnesota, 1971.

Donaldson, George W., and Swan, Malcolm D. *Administration of Eco-Education*. Washington, D.C.: AAHPER, 1201 Sixteenth Street N.W., 1979.

Fluegelman, Andrew. *More New Games*. New York: Dolphin Books, Doubleday, 1981.

Fluegelman, Andrew, ed. *The New Games Book*. New York: Dolphin Books, Doubleday, 1976.

Ford, Phyllis M. *Principles and Practices of Outdoor/Environmental Education*. New York: John Wiley and Sons, 1981.

Gabrielson, Alexander M., and Holtzer, Charles. *The Role of Outdoor Education*. New York: Center for Applied Research in Education, 1965.

Gross, Phyllis, and Railton, Esther P. *Teaching Science in an Outdoor Environment*. Berkeley: University of California Press, 1972.

Hammerman, Donald R.; Hammerman, William M.; and Hammerman, Elizabeth L. *Teaching in the Outdoors*. Danville, Ill.: Interstate Printers and Publishers, 1985.

Hammerman, William M., ed. *Fifty Years of Resident Outdoor Education: 1930-1980*. Martinsville, Ind.: American Camping Association, 1980.

Hawkins, Donald E., and Vinton, Dennis. *The Environmental Classroom*. Englewood Cliffs, N.J.: Prentice-Hall, 1973.

Hug, John W., and Wilson, Phyllis J. *Curriculum Enrichment Outdoors*. New York: Harper & Row, 1965.

Knapp, Clifford E. *Humanizing Environmental Education: A Guide for Leading Nature and Human Nature Activities.* Martinsville, Ind.: American Camping Association, 1981.

Link, Michael. *Outdoor Education: A Manual for Teaching in Nature's Classroom.* Englewood Cliffs, N.J.: Prentice-Hall, 1981.

Marsh, Norman F. *Outdoor Education on Your School Ground.* Sacramento: State of California Resources Agency, 1967.

McInnis, Noel, and Albrecht, Don, ed. *What Makes Education Environmental?* Louisville, Ky.: Data Courier, 1975.

Smith, Julian, et. al. *Outdoor Education.* Englewood Cliffs, N.J.: Prentice-Hall, n.d.

Staley, Frederick A. *Outdoor Education for the Whole Child.* Dubuque, Iowa: Kendall/Hunt, 1979.

Stapp, William B., and Cox, Dorothy A. *Environmental Education Activities Manual.* Farmington Hills, Mich.: William B. Stapp and Dorothy Cox, Publishers, 1974.

Swan, Malcolm D., ed. *Tips and Tricks in Outdoor Education.* Danville, Ill.: Interstate Printers and Publishers, 1978.

van der Smissen, Betty, and Goering, Oswald H. *Nature-Oriented Activities.* Ames: Iowa State University Press, 1980.

Van Matre, Steve. *Sunship Earth: An Acclimatization Program for Outdoor Learning.* Martinsville, Ind.: American Camping Association, 1979.

Van Matre, Steve. *Acclimatizing: A Personal and Reflective Approach to a Natural Relationship.* Martinsville, Ind.: American Camping Association, 1974.

Van Matre, Steve. *Acclimatization: A Sensory and Conceptual Approach to Ecological Involvement.* Martinsville, Ind.: American Camping Association, 1972.

Vivian, Eugene, and Rillo, Thomas J. *Focus on Environmental Education.* Glassboro: Curriculum Development Council for Southern New Jersey, 1970.

Wheatly, John H., and Coon, Herbert L. *Teaching Activities in Environmental Education.* Vol. 2 and 3. ERIC. Columbus: Ohio State University, 1974 and 1975.

Wurman, Richard S., ed. *Yellow Pages of Learning Resources.* Cambridge, Mass.: M.I.T. Press, 1972.

Periodicals

Journal of Environmental Education. Published four times a year by Heldref Publications, 4000 Albemarle Street N.W., Washington, DC 20016, this journal is addressed to teachers on all levels; education specialists in museums, zoos, parks, refuges, camps, clubs, historic sites, societies; and specialists in extension, adult, and non-traditional education programs. It is a valuable resource for educators concerned with the problems of the socio-cultural and biophysical environment.

Journal of Experiential Education. The official publication of the Association for Experiential Education, 7200 E. Dry Creek Road, Suite F 203, Englewood, CO 80112, this journal advances the cause of experiential education for learners of all ages.

Journal of Outdoor Education. Published once each academic year at the Lorado Taft Field Campus of Northern Illinois University, Box 299, Oregon, IL 61061, this journal is distributed free of charge to interested individuals as well as libraries and institutions. It has included articles on adventure programming, stress-challenge, Canadian outdoor education, and outdoor education in other countries, and other topics useful to the classroom teacher and full-time outdoor educator.

The Outdoor Communicator. Published quarterly by the New York State Outdoor Education Association, 196 Morton Avenue, Albany, NY 12202, it contains many practical articles useful to the practitioner in the field as well as the classroom teacher.

Science Activities. Published quarterly by Heldref Publications, 4000 Albemarle Street N.W., Washington DC 20016, it is a source of experiments, explorations, projects, and outdoor field studies that have been teacher-tested. Each issue contains a variety of activities for the young child up to the advanced high school student. The journal is especially useful for the classroom teacher and for preservice or inservice programs on the use of the outdoor laboratory.

Modular Resources

American Forest Institute. *Project Learning Tree.* 2 volumes. Washington, D.C., 1977.

National Education Association. *Man and His Environment (NEED).* Washington, D.C., 1970.

Green Box. Eureka, Calif.: Humboldt County Office of Education, Environmental Education Program, 1975.

Outdoor Biological Instructional Strategies (OBIS). Berkeley: Regents of the University of California, 1975.

U.S. Forest Service. *Understanding Your Environment Series.* Portland, Oregon, n.d.

Western Regional Environmental Education Council. *Project Wild.* Volume 1, *Elementary Activity Guide*, and Volume 2, *Secondary Activity Guide.* Boulder, Colo., 1983.